Wri

Pocket Booster

OCR Gateway A
Biology 1, 2 and 3

For GCSE Biology
Higher Tier

Subscribe to Wright Science on YouTube to for a full set of videos to support you in your GCSE science studies.

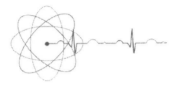

WRIGHT SCIENCE

SCIENCE DONE THE WRIGHT WAY

ISBN: 9781717843241

2018

How to use this pocket booster

Each topic has a QR code at the end of the page. If you download a free QR code reader on your phone, this will then take you to the video about that topic on YouTube.

At the end of each section, there are some quick questions to check your understanding.

The key idea of this book is to carry it with you and just take those few minutes in a queue or on the bus to read a couple of pages to check you know it. Learn it, revisit it and then review it again. The more you do this, the more information you will retain.

I hope that you find this book useful.

For SW for putting up with my many hours at a computer in the name of teaching science.

B1
Cell Level
Systems

B1.1.1: Cell Structures

There are two main types of cell:

- Prokaryotic cells (bacterial)
- Eukaryotic cells (plant and animal)

Prokaryotic	Eukaryotic
No nucleus	Nucleus containing genetic material
Simple	Complex
1μm to 10μm	10μm to 100μm

Maths reminder: 1mm = 1000μm

Eukaryotic Cells

All eukaryotic cells have four parts:
- Nucleus
- Cytoplasm
- Cell membrane
- Mitochondria

Animal Cell

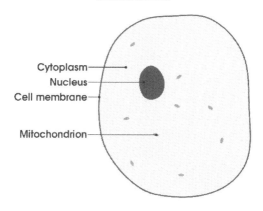

Cytoplasm
Nucleus
Cell membrane
Mitochondrion

Plant Cell

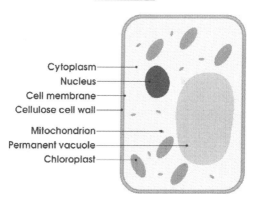

Cytoplasm
Nucleus
Cell membrane
Cellulose cell wall
Mitochondrion
Permanent vacuole
Chloroplast

Prokaryotic Cell

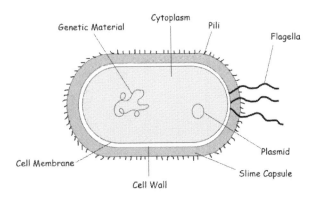

All prokaryotic cells contain:
- Cell Membrane
- Cell Wall
- Genetic Material
- Cytoplasm

Some prokaryotic cells contain:
- Pili
- Flagella
- Slime Capsule
- Plasmid

Bacteria are unicellular (one cell). They are the smallest living organisms as they can carry out all seven life processes:

- Movement
- Respiration
- Sensitivity
- Growth
- Reproduction
- Excretion
- Nutrition

Exam hint: Remember the life processes using a pneumonic like MRS GREN.

Three examples of bacteria:

- *E.coli*
- *Streptococcus*
- *Streptomyces*

Subcellular Structure	Function
Nucleus (A,P)	Controls the cell and contains genetic material
Cytoplasm (A,P,Pr)	Site of chemical reactions
Cell membrane (A,P,Pr)	Controls what enters and leaves the cell, contains receptor molecules
Mitochondria (A,P)	Contains enzymes for respiration, site of respiration
Cell Wall (P,Pr)	Supports the cell. Cellulose in plants; peptidoglycan in prokaryotes
Vacuole (P)	Contains cell sap and helps support the plant
Chloroplast (P)	Contain chlorophyll to trap light energy for photosynthesis
Free Genetic	Circular strand of DNA

Material (Pr)	found in the cytoplasm, contains the genes
Flagella (Pr)	Allow the cell to move
Pili (Pr)	Allow the cell to attach to surfaces and cells, transfer of genetic material
Slime Capsule (Pr)	Protects the cell and helps it stick to smooth surfaces
Plasmid (Pr)	Circular DNA that stores extra genes

A = Animal; P = Plant; Pr = Prokaryotic

B1.1.2: Light Microscopy

Uses light to view a specimen.

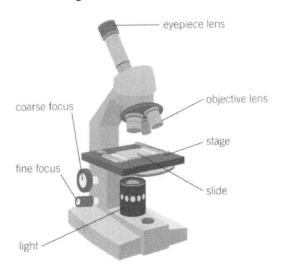

Total magnification = Eyepiece lens
magnification x Objective lens
magnification

Actual size = Measured size ÷
Magnification

PAG B1: Microscopy

1. Move the stage to its lowest position.
2. Select the objective lens with the lowest magnification
3. Place the slide onto the stage.
4. Turn the coarse focus knob slowly until you see your object.
5. Turn the fine focus know slowly until the object becomes clear.
6. Repeat steps 4 and 5 using the higher magnification objective lens to see more detail.

Use a sharp pencil and single lines (no artistic sketchy lines!)
Use at least half the space given.
Always write the magnification.
Label lines drawn with a ruler.
Labels to the side of the drawing.

Many cells are colourless. Stains are used to make them more visible by colouring the cell. Some stains colour the whole cell, and others highlight specific subcellular structures.

Methylene blue – Makes the nucleus easier to see in animal cells.
Iodine: Makes the nucleus easier to see in plant cells.
Crystal violet: Stains bacterial cell walls.

To apply a stain:
1. Place the cells on a slide.
2. Add one drop of stain using a pipette.
3. Place a coverslip on top and gently lower it with a needle.
4. Tap coverslip gently to remove air bubbles.

B1.1.3: Electron Microscopy

Resolution: The smallest distance between two points that can still be seen as separate entities.

Structures smaller than $0.2\mu m$ cannot be seen with a light microscope.

Electron microscopes use fast moving electrons. The electrons are emitted from the source in a vacuum. The lenses are replaced by coil-shaped electromagnets which bend the electron beams. This produces an electron micrograph.

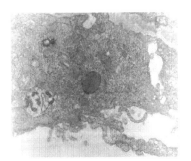

Electron microscopes:

- Let us see more detail
- Reveal greater information on subcellular structures
- Understand the structure of viruses to help develop drugs.

There are two types of electron microscope:

1. Transmission Electron Microscope (TEM) – produce the most magnified images.
2. Scanning Electron Microscope (SEM) – produce 3D images of the surface.

Comparing light and electron microscopes:

Light Microscope	Electron Microscope
Cheap	Expensive
Small	Large
Portable	Difficult to move
Simple sample preparation	Complex sample preparation
$0.2\mu m$ resolution $(2.0 \times 10^{-7}m)$	$0.1nm$ resolution $(1.0 \times 10^{-10}m)$
Living or dead specimens	Dead specimens
Natural colour seen unless stained	Black and white images

Check Your Knowledge

1. Name the four parts of an animal cell.

2. Which subcellular structures are present in a plant cell but not an animal cell?

3. Name three parts of a prokaryotic cell.

4. List three differences between light microscopes and electron microscopes.

5. Why do we stain cells?

6. Describe how to view an onion cell.

B1.2.1: DNA

Genetic material in eukaryotic cells:
- DNA is found in the nucleus.
- It is organised into structures called chromosomes.
- Sections of the DNA on the chromosome are called genes and they code for a protein.

Everyone's DNA is unique except for identical twins.

Genes are short sections of DNA that code for a certain characteristic. E.g. hair colour
They code for proteins.

Not all genes are switched on in all cells. Some genes are switched off to stop them making that protein.

DNA is a polymer made up of two stands which are bonded together to form a double helix.

The strands are made of monomers called nucleotides.

A nucleotide is made up of:
Sugar: Deoxyribose
Phosphate
Base: Adenine, Thymine, Cytosine or Guanine

Block diagram of nucleotide:

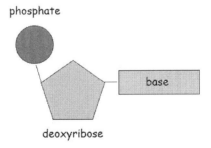

phosphate

base

deoxyribose

The nucleotides join together to make a sugar-phosphate backbone.

The bases then bond via complementary base pairing to connect the two strands of DNA to make the double helix.

A to T
C to G

Protein Synthesis

DNA is used to make proteins in a process called protein synthesis. This process has two parts:

Part 1: Transcription

The required gene is copied:
- DNA unzips
- Free RNA bases pair in complementary pairs to make mRNA. (RNA does not have thymine, it is replaced with uracil, U).
- mRNA detaches from the DNA and leaves the nucleus where it travels to a ribosome.

Part 2: Translation

- mRNA attaches to a ribosome.
- The mRNA bases are read in triplets.
- Each triplet codes for an amino acid.
- Each amino acid is joined together to make a polymer chain.
- The sequence of amino acids determines how the protein will fold.

B1.2.2: Enzymes

Enzymes are made of protein. This means they are made of long chains of amino acids.

These fold up in a specific shape. The area at which the substrate binds to the enzyme is called the active site.

They are biological catalysts. This means they speed up chemical reactions in living organisms.

Enzymes can either build large molecules from small ones or break large molecules into smaller ones.

Enzymes are specific. This means the active site will only bind with one substrate.
The lock and key hypothesis explains this.

The enzyme-substrate complex is formed when the substrate binds to the active site.
The products are released from the enzyme once the reaction has taken place. The enzyme can then catalyse another reaction.

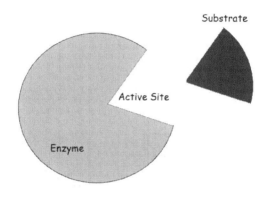

The rate at which an enzyme-catalysed reaction occurs depends upon:
- Temperature
- pH
- Substrate concentration
- Enzyme concentration

Factor 1: Temperature

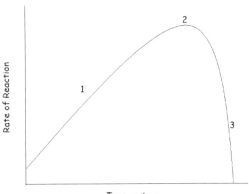

1: When the temperature increases, particles gain kinetic energy so they move faster and are more likely to collide. This leads to an increased rate of reaction with increasing temperature.

2: The optimum is the fastest rate for the enzyme.

3: Beyond the optimum, increasing the temperature breaks bonds within the protein which leads to the active site changing shape. This is denaturing. The substrate no longer fits.

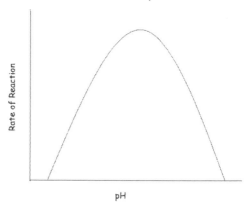

Each enzyme has an optimum pH. This depends on its intended location of function.

E.g. An enzyme in the stomach will have an optimum pH of around pH2.

If the pH is too acidic or alkaline, the enzyme is denatured.

Factor 3: Concentration of Substrate

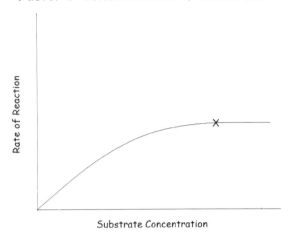

Substrate Concentration

As the concentration of substrate increases, the chance of a collision between the enzyme and substrate also increases.

When you reach the saturation point (X), the rate plateaus as all the enzymes are bound to a substrate at any given time.

Factor 4: Concentration of Enzyme

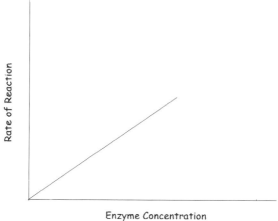

As the concentration of enzyme increases, the chance of a collision between the enzyme and substrate also increases.

You eventually react a point where there is a surplus of enzymes compared to the substrate so there is no further increase.

PAG B4: Enzymes

Variables: Anything that can change in the experiment. (Times; Temperatures; Amounts etc)
Controlled variables: Factors which have been kept the same.
Independent Variable: Factor we are changing.
Dependent variable: Factor we are measuring.

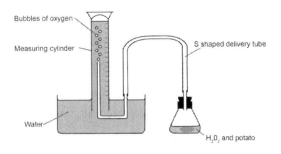

Calculating rate of reaction:
Volume of gas / Time

If in the experiment, the enzyme is breaking down a complex molecule:

Starch is broken down into glucose (Benedict's test to test for sugars or iodine to test for starch)

Protein is broken down into amino acids (Biuret Test to test for proteins)

Fats are broken down into fatty acids and glycerol (Ethanol test to test for fats)

Potential Improvements:
Use a gas syringe as it gives more precise readings/more accurate scale for measuring gas volume.

Use a water bath to provide a constant temperature throughout the experiment.

Check Your Knowledge

1. What is a biological catalyst?

2. Which part of the enzyme does the substrate bind to?

3. What is denaturing?

4. Explain how temperature affects enzyme activity.

5. Explain how pH affects enzyme activity.

6. How can you measure the volume of gas produced in an experiment?

B1.3.1: Aerobic Respiration

Metabolic Rate

The metabolic rate is the speed at which your body uses energy. This will be different in different people and impacts the amount of food you need to eat.

The food you eat is made up of:

1) Carbohydrates are polymers made from simple sugars. They are broken down by carbohydrase enzymes and used for energy.

2) Proteins are polymers made from amino acids. The sequence of amino acids determines what protein is made. They are broken down by protease enzymes and used in growth and repair.

3) Lipids are made from three fatty acids joined to a glycerol molecule. They are broken down by lipase enzymes and are used for energy, buoyancy and insulation. When broken down, the pH decreases as fatty acids are released.

Aerobic Respiration

Respiration occurs all the time to provide energy. It takes place inside the mitochondria as they contain the enzymes needed.

Different cells have different numbers of mitochondria which depends on the function of the cell.

Liver and muscle cells have lots of mitochondria as they need lots of energy.

Aerobic respiration is a series of chemical reactions controlled by enzymes that can be simplified to:

Word Equation:
Glucose + Oxygen → Carbon Dioxide + Water

Balanced Symbol Equation:
$C_6H_{12}O_6 + 6O_2 \rightarrow 6CO_2 + 6H_2O$

Exam hint: If they ask you to balance this equation...Just remember 666.

This is an exothermic reaction.

Aerobic respiration produces 38 molecules of ATP which is used for movement, to stay warm and to build large molecules.

B1.3.2: Anaerobic Respiration

When there is a lack of oxygen, anaerobic respiration occurs.

Glucose → Lactic Acid

Lactic acid is toxic and causes muscle fatigue and cramps.

Oxygen is needed to break down the lactic acid. This oxygen is called the oxygen debt. This is why you keep breathing faster and your heart rate stays higher after exercise.

Anaerobic respiration only produces 2 ATP molecules.

It is used to transfer energy quickly and provide energy when oxygen is not available.

Fermentation

Glucose → Ethanol + Carbon Dioxide

$$C_6H_{12}O_6 \rightarrow 2C_2H_5OH + 2CO_2$$

This process is carried out by yeast to make ethanol.

Check Your Knowledge

1. What is the name of the enzyme that breaks down carbohydrates?

2. What are the monomers of proteins?

3. Why does the pH drop when lipids are broken down?

4. What is the word equation for aerobic respiration?

5. What is the balanced symbol equation for aerobic respiration?

6. Compare aerobic and anaerobic respiration.

B1.4.1: Photosynthesis

Photosynthetic organisms are the main producers of food and biomass on Earth.

Photosynthesis takes place inside the chloroplasts. These are mainly found inside the leaves and the stem (the green bits of the plant).

The chloroplasts contain the green pigment called chlorophyll which traps light energy from the sun.

Plants also take in carbon dioxide from the air through the stomata by diffusion and water which enters the roots by osmosis.

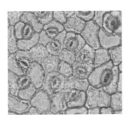

Photosynthesis is a two stage process:

Stage 1: Light dependent
Energy from the light is used to split water molecules into oxygen and hydrogen ions.

Stage 2: Light independent
Carbon dioxide combines with the hydrogen ions to make glucose.

Carbon Dioxide + Water → Glucose + Oxygen

$$6CO_2 + 6H_2O \rightarrow C_6H_{12}O_6 + 6O_2$$

Exam hint: If you know photosynthesis, you know aerobic respiration as they are the inverse of each other.

Photosynthesis is an endothermic reaction.

The glucose made is used in a range of ways:
- Converted into starch as a food store
- Converted into cellulose to form cell walls
- Used in respiration
- Converted into proteins by having nitrogen added

Photosynthesis Experiments

Scientists have carried out experiments over the years to provide us with the understanding of the process of photosynthesis.

Joseph Priestley carried out experiments on mice in bell jars to prove a gas was produced by plants that animals needed to live in 1772.

Jan Ingenhousz discovered that green plants give off bubbles in the light which he identified as oxygen. He also discovered that plants give off carbon dioxide in the dark. His observations proved that some of the mass in plants comes from the air as well as the water and soil.

PAG B5: Photosynthesis

We can carry out a range of experiments to test different aspects of photosynthesis.

One key aspect of these experiments is how to test the leaf for starch:
1. Take a leaf and place it in boiling water for 1 minute to kill it.
2. Place the leaf in a boiling tube containing ethanol to remove the chlorophyll.
3. Place the tube containing the ethanol and leaf in a beaker of boiling water for 5 minutes (No open flames as ethanol is flammable)
4. Wash the leaf with water and spread it out on a white tile.
5. Add a few drops of iodine solution.
6. If iodine goes blue-black, starch is present.

Before we carry out any experiments on photosynthesis, we need to destarch the plant by placing in the dark for 24 hours or more.

To prove chlorophyll is needed

Destarch a variegated plant.
Place the plant in sunlight for several hours.
Test the leaf for starch.

To prove light is needed:
Destarch a plant.
Cover part of a leaf with black card or tin foil.
Place in sunlight for several hours.
Remove the card and test the leaf for starch.

To prove carbon dioxide is needed:
Destarch a plant.
Cover with a polythene bag and add a pot of soda lime.
Place in sunlight for several hours.
Test a leaf for starch.

To prove oxygen is given off:
Place pondweed in a beaker.
Collect the gas made,
Test for oxygen (glowing splint relights).

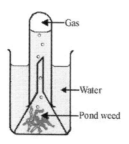

To investigate how light intensity
alters the rate of photosynthesis:

1. Place the pondweed in a beaker of
    dilute sodium hydrogen carbonate
    solution.
2. Place the lamp 10cm from the beaker.
3. Count the bubbles produced in 1
    minute.
4. Move the lamp 10cm further away and
    repeat.

Problems:

1. Lamp heats up the water increasing
    the rate of photosynthesis as it is an
    enzyme controlled reaction.

2. Counting bubbles is inaccurate – miss
    one, bubbles have different volumes.

Improvements:

1. Place a beaker of water between the lamp and beaker with pondweed to act as a heat shield.

2. Use an upturned measuring cylinder or a gas syringe to collect the gas and record a volume.

Inverse Square Law

When you double the distance from a light source, the light intensity increases by a factor of 4.

Relative light intensity = $1 \div d^2$
(d = distance from light source)

B1.4.2: Factors Affecting Photosynthesis

The factors which affect the rate of photosynthesis are called limiting factors. They are:

Light Intensity

The higher the light intensity, the faster the rate of photosynthesis.

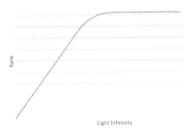

The graph levels off as light is no longer the limiting factor.

Carbon Dioxide Concentration

The higher the concentration of carbon dioxide, the faster the rate of photosynthesis.

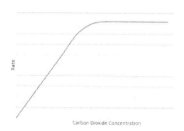

The graph levels off as carbon dioxide concentration is no longer the limiting factor.

Temperature

Photosynthesis is an enzyme controlled reaction.

As the temperature increases, the rate increases as the particles have more kinetic energy and are more likely to collide and react.

After the optimum has been exceeded, the enzymes denature and the active site has changed shape so the reaction can no longer occur.

Check Your Knowledge

1. List the limiting factors of photosynthesis.

2. Explain how temperature affects the rate of photosynthesis.

3. Explain why the graph of rate of photosynthesis against light intensity levels off.

4. What is the inverse square law?

5. What is the word equation and balanced symbol equation for photosynthesis?

6. What is destarching?

B2
Scaling Up

B2.1.1: Diffusion

Diffusion: The net movement of particles from an area of high concentration to an area of low concentration.

They move down a concentration gradient.

It is a passive process.

This continues until the concentration gradient is zero.

Diffusion is the process by which particles enter and leave cells.

There are three factors that affect the rate of diffusion:

1.   Distance:
The larger the distance, the slower the rate of diffusion. It takes longer to travel larger distances.

Capillaries are only one cell thick to make the diffusion distance as short as possible.

2.   Concentration Gradient:
The steeper the concentration gradient, the faster the rate of diffusion.

3. Surface Area:
The greater the surface area, the faster the rate of diffusion. There is more space for diffusion to occur over.

This is why the lungs have alveoli and the small intestines have villi.

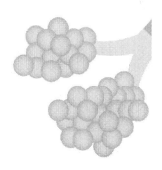

B2.1.2: Osmosis

Osmosis: The movement of water molecules from an area of high water potential to an area of lower water potential (down a concentration gradient) across a selectively permeable membrane.

The greater the difference in water potential, the greater the rate of osmosis.

Plant Cells:

If the solution has a higher water potential than the cells, water enters the cell by osmosis. This increases the turgor pressure and the cell becomes turgid.

If the solution has the same water potential as the cells, there is no net movement of water.

If the solution has a lower water potential than the cells, water leaves the cell by osmosis. This decreases the turgor pressure and the cell becomes flaccid. Eventually the cell membrane pulls away from the cell wall and the cell becomes plasmolysed.

Animal Cells:

If the solution has a higher water potential than the cells, water enters the cell by osmosis. This makes the cell swell and then burst (lysis).

If the solution has the same water potential as the cells, there is no net movement of water.

If the solution has a lower water potential than the cells, water leaves the cell by osmosis. The cell becomes crenated (crinkled).

PAG B8: Osmosis

This experiment is usually carried out with either potato or carrot. The solution can be made with either salt or sugar.

Method:
1. Cut the chips of potato.
2. Record their start mass.
3. Place them in a beaker with enough solution to cover the chip.
4. Leave for 15 minutes.
5. Remove the chips from the solution and record their end mass.
6. Calculate the percentage change in mass.

Percentage Change =
$$\frac{\text{Final Mass} - \text{Start Mass}}{\text{Start Mass}} \times 100$$

Positive means it gained mass.
Negative means it lost mass.
Sources of Error and Solutions:
Moisture on the surface increasing mass –
Dry the chip before re-weighing.

Using change in length – Only takes one
dimension into consideration. Change in
mass is better.

Chip not covered by solution so it dries
out – Ensure the chip is covered.

Balance shows no change in mass –
Accuracy of the balance may be too low
so select a balance with more than one
decimal place.

B2.1.3: Active Transport

Active Transport: The movement of substances from an area of low concentration to an area of high concentration. They move against the concentration gradient.

This requires energy in the form of ATP. It is an active process.

Cells that carry out a lot of active transport have more mitochondria present.

It also requires carrier proteins spanning the cell membrane.

Examples of active transport include glucose in the small intestine; root hair cells and nerve cells.

How carrier proteins work:

Molecule binds to specific carrier proteins.

ATP is used to change the shape of the protein and the molecule is transported across the membrane.

B2.1.4: Mitosis

Body cells must divide for repair, replacement and growth.

Body cells divide by mitosis.

Mitosis produces two genetically identical daughter cells (clones).

The cell cycle is the process of cell growth and division. There are four stages:

1. DNA replication
2. Movement of chromosomes
3. Cytokinesis
4. Growth of daughter cell

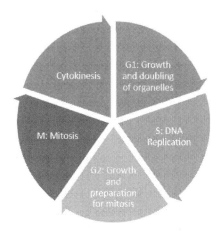

DNA Replication:
The DNA unzips and free bases pair up
with their complementary base pairs: A-T
and C-G.

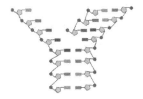

Chromosome Movement:

The chromosomes line up along the equator and are pulled apart to opposite poles of the cell. A new nucleus forms around the new sets of chromosomes.

Cytokinesis:

The cell membrane pinches in and the two daughter cells split from each other.

Growth:

The cells grow. Once fully grown, the cell cycle starts again.

B2.1.5: Cell Differentiation

Differentiation: Conversion of an unspecialised cell to become specialised to carry out a particular function.

Sperm Cells:
- Flagellum to move the sperm
- Lots of mitochondria to provide energy
- Acrosome contains digestive enzymes to break down the egg membrane to allow the sperm to enter.

Red Blood Cells:
- Biconcave disc shape to increase the surface area to volume ratio to increase the rate of diffusion.
- Contain haemoglobin to bind to oxygen.
- No nucleus to for more haemoglobin.

B2.1.6: Stem Cells

Stem cells are undifferentiated cells.

They can divide by mitosis and then differentiate into any type of specialised cell.

There are two types:
1. Adult Stem Cells:
Found in tissues like bone marrow, skin and liver.
They are used to repair damage. They can only differentiate into some cell types.

2. Embryonic Stem Cells:
Found in embryos and can differentiate into any cell type.

Embryonic stem cells are used in research and may have the potential to cure certain diseases.

Plants grow throughout their lives in the meristems. These are found in the root tips, shoot tips and buds.

Meristem cells are small with very thin cell walls and no chloroplasts.

Check Your Knowledge

1. Define the terms: Diffusion, osmosis and active transport.

2. Explain what happens when a plant cell is placed in a concentrated sugar solution.

3. Describe the process of mitosis.

4. How do carrier proteins work.

5. Define the term stem cell.

6. What are the stem cells in plants called?

7. Explain how a sperm cell is specialised.

B2.2.1: Exchange and Transport

Surface area to volume ratio is the surface area per unit volume of an object.

It is important in living organisms. e.g. tapeworms have a large surface area to volume ratio to absorb the nutrients it needs to keep it alive.

The larger the organism, the lower the surface area to volume ratio becomes. There comes a time when the organism is too big to get all it needs by diffusion alone as it is too slow. To overcome this problem, multicellular organisms have developed adaptations to increase surface area to volume ratio at exchange surfaces.
E.g. lungs with alveoli; Intestines with villi and microvilli

B2.2.2: The Circulatory System

The circulatory system is made of the heart, arteries, veins and capillaries.

It is a double circulatory system as blood flows through the heart twice on one circuit round the body so it is pumped twice by the heart. The blood is under a higher pressure than in a single circulatory system.

The human circulatory system is known as a closed system. This is because the blood remains within vessels the whole time.

There are three types of blood vessel:
1. Arteries (Away from the heart)
2. Veins (Back to the heart)
3. Capillaries (Exchanges)

Arteries have a thick muscular and elastic wall to withstand the high pressure of blood leaving the heart.

The wall expands with the force of each contraction and recoils to push the blood forward.

Veins have a thinner wall and larger lumen than arteries. The blood is under lower pressure. They also contain valves to stop the backflow of blood.

Capillaries have a wall only one cell thick to make diffusion happen faster.

B2.2.3: Blood

1. Red blood cells:
Transport oxygen using biconcave disc shape to increase SA:V ratio; contain carrier protein haemoglobin; have no nucleus to carry more haemoglobin.

2. White blood cells:
Fight infections by engulfing and digesting pathogens or making antibodies.

3. Plasma:
Straw coloured liquid that carries hormones, antibodies and wastes.

4. Platelets:
Help blood to clot to reduce blood loss and chances of infection.

B2.2.4: The Heart

The heart is made of cardiac muscle which contracts without a nerve impulse from the brain.

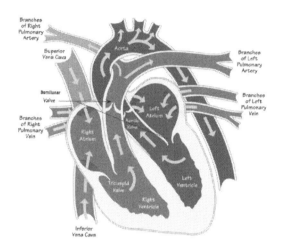

The heart has 4 chambers: 2 atria (at the top) and 2 ventricles (at the bottom).

Valves stop the backflow of blood.

Left side has a thicker muscle wall than the right as it has to pump blood all the way around the body.

The right side only has to go to the lungs so has a thinner muscle wall. This means the right side has blood under a lower pressure to prevent lung tissue being damaged.

B2.2.5: Plant Transport Systems

Plants have two tissues to transport substances.

The xylem transports water and dissolved mineral ions from the roots to the stem, leaves and flowers. (Think WXY)

Water enters the roots via osmosis. Mineral ions are taken up by active transport.

Xylem is made from dead cells with no end walls between them. Lignin has been used to thicken the walls and provide support.

Phloem transports the dissolved sugars made in photosynthesis around the plant.

Translocation: The movement of dissolved sugars and other food molecules.

Sugars are taken to the meristems where they are used to make new cells or the roots for storage.

Phloem is made of living cells with sieve plates as the end walls. The sugars are able to pass through the sieve plates.

The xylem and phloem are packaged together in a structure called the vascular bundle. The location of the vascular bundle is different in different parts of the plant:
- In the leaf: Form a network to support soft tissue.
- In the stem: Around the outside to provide strength.
- In the root: In the centre to let the root bend.

B2.2.6: The Transpiration Stream

Transpiration: Loss of water vapour from the aerial parts of the plant. (Leaves)

Transpiration Stream: The movement of water from the roots, through the xylem and out of the leaves.

Any water lost from the leaves has to be replaced by uptake through the roots.

Water enters the root hair cells by osmosis and travels from cell to cell until it reaches the xylem in the middle of the root. From here, it is transported through the plant.

The leaves have stomata present on their surface which allow carbon dioxide to diffuse into the plant. The guard cells control the opening and closing of the stomata.

When they are open, water evaporates from the cells inside the leaf into the air spaces.

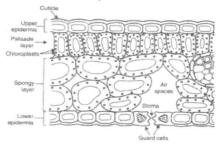

This creates a concentration gradient between the inside and outside of the leaves.

Water vapour moves down the concentration gradient and diffuses out of the plant into the air.

The loss of water in the leaves reduces the pressure in the xylem vessel in the leaf so water moves down a pressure gradient from the roots to the leaves.

To reduce water loss, leaves are covered with a waxy cuticle.

If a plant loses water faster than it is taken in, the plant will wilt. This makes the leaves collapse and droop so the surface area for evaporation is reduced.

The stomata will close but this limits the rate of photosynthesis as no carbon dioxide can be taken in.

B2.2.7: Factors Affecting Transpiration

To measure the rate of transpiration, we can use a potometer.

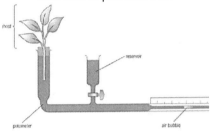

1. Take an air bubble into the capillary tube.
2. As the water moves into the shoot and evaporates, the air bubble will move towards the plant.
3. The distance over a certain time can be measured to let us calculate the speed.

There are four factors which affect the rate of transpiration.

Temperature:
As you increase the temperature, water evaporates faster from the leaf. Diffusion of water vapour out of the leaf becomes faster so the rate of transpiration increases.

Air Movement:
As air moves over the surface of the leaf, evaporated water molecules are moved away. The faster the air moves, the faster the water molecules are carried away. This increases the concentration gradient between the leaf and air so water diffuses out faster.

Light Intensity:
Stomata open in the light and close in the dark. Increasing the light intensity will lead to more water evaporating. Transpiration reaches a maximum rate when all stomata are open.

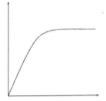

Humidity:
Decreasing the humidity will create a steeper concentration gradient so will lead to a faster rate of transpiration.

B3
Organism Level Systems

B3.1.1: The Nervous System

Stimulus: Change in the environment.

Receptors: Cells that detect the stimulus and change it into electrical impulses which travel along neurones.

Response occurs at the effectors. Muscles will contract and glands will release hormones.

Central Nervous System (CNS): Brain and spinal cord

The CNS is made of delicate nervous tissue which is protected by the skull and vertebral column.

There are three types of neurones:

1. Sensory: From receptor cells to the CNS.

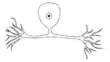

2. Relay: From the sensory neurone to motor neurone.

3. Motor: From the relay neurone to the effector.

A nervous reaction takes around 0.7s and follows the pathway:
Stimulus → Receptor → Sensory Neurone → Spinal Cord → Brain → Spinal Cord → Motor Neurone → Effector → Response

The brain receives vast amounts of information from the sensory receptors at the same time and processes the information to form a coordinated response. This results in impulses being sent to different parts of the body.

B3.1.2: Reflexes

You have two types of response in your body: Voluntary and Involuntary.

Reflex actions are involuntary and take around 0.2s.

The reflex arc is:

Stimulus → Receptor → Sensory Neurone → Relay Neurone → Motor Neurone → Effector → Response

B3.1.3: The Eye

Structure	Function
Cornea	Protect the eye, refract light
Pupil	Allows light to enter the eye
Iris	Alters the pupil size by contracting and relaxing
Lens	Focuses the light onto the retina
Ciliary Muscle	Alters the shape of the lens
Suspensory Ligaments	Connects the ciliary muscle to the lens
Optic Nerve	Carries nerve impulses to the brain

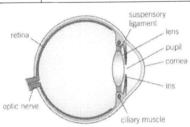

The cornea refracts the light to focus the incoming light. The light passes through the pupil and is further refracted by the lens. This creates a sharp image on the retina. The photoreceptors in the retina produce a nervous impulse which travels down the optic nerve to the brain.

To focus on objects at different distances, the lens has to change shape.

The ciliary muscle contracts to make the lens more convex to focus on near objects.

The ciliary muscle relaxes to make the lens more convex to focus on far objects.

Problems of vision
Short sightedness is where distant objects appear blurry. It is corrected with a concave lens.

Long sightedness is where near objects appear blurry. It is corrected with a convex lens.

Colour blindness is where people have difficulty making out different colours. The most common form is red-green colour blindness. This is a genetic condition that usually affects males.

The retina has two types of photoreceptor cell.

Rods: Allow you to see in low light intensity but do not respond to different colours.

Cones: Respond to different colours. Different cone cells respond to red, blue and green light.

B3.1.4: The Brain

The brain processes all the information collected by receptor cells about internal and external environmental changes along with information from the hormonal system.

It produces a coordinated response using all the information.

Having the brain as a central control centre makes the process faster than if different functions were controlled in different regions of the body.

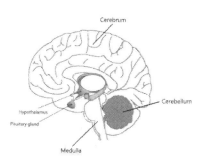

The 5 main areas of the brain are:

1. Cerebrum: Controls complex behaviour (learning, memory, personality and conscious thought)
2. Hypothalamus: Regulates temperature and water balance.
3. Cerebellum: Controls posture, balance and involuntary movements.
4. Medulla: Controls automatic actions (heart rate, breathing rate)
5. Pituitary gland: Stores and releases hormones that regulate many body functions.

Investigating brain function is difficult. It requires consent from patients and to draw reliable conclusions, many cases need to be analysed. When investigating a specific function, there may be multiple regions of the brain involved. If considering animal testing, many people think this is unethical.

These days we have a range of scans which allow brain function to be investigated. These include:

CT scans which use X-rays to produce 3D images of the brain.

MRI scans which use powerful magnets to identify anomalies.

fMRI scans which show areas of the brain with increased blood flow.

Through the use of these new technologies, we have a greater understanding of the brain.

B3.1.5: Nervous System Damage

The nervous system is divided into two sections:

CNS: Brain and spinal cord
PNS: All the neurones that connect the CNS to the rest of the body.

Nervous system damage could be caused by:
- Injury
- Genetic Condition (Huntington's Disease)
- Disease
- Toxic substances being consumed (Lead)

Damage to the nervous system prevents impulses being passed effectively through the nervous system.

Damage to the PNS can affect sensory and motor neurones resulting in:

- Numbness
- Inability to detect pain
- Loss of coordination

Minor damage to the PNS can self-heal.

Damage to the CNS is more severe and can lead to:

- Loss of control of body systems
- Partial or complete paralysis
- Memory loss or processing difficulties

CNS cannot regenerate so damage is permanent unless surgery can correct it.

The spinal cord is difficult to repair as individual nerve fibres are surrounded by many others that could be damaged.

Brain damage is difficult to diagnose. Limited treatments are available and include:

- Radiotherapy or chemotherapy for tumours.

- Surgery to remove damaged tissue.

- Deep brain stimulation using electrodes.

Check Your Understanding

1. What are the three types of neurone?

2. What is a coordinated response?

3. What are effectors?

4. List the order of the reflex arc?

5. Explain how you focus on a near object.

6. Name the five regions of the brain and their function.

7. Explain the impacts of nervous system damage and how it can be treated.

B3.2.1: Hormones

A hormone is a chemical messenger which is made in the endocrine glands. They travel through the blood in the plasma until they reach the target organs where they cause a response.

Hormones	Nervous
Fairly slow	Fast
Long lasting	Short lasting
Chemicals in blood	Electrical impulse along axon of neurone
Large area targeted	Precise area targeted

Homeostasis: The maintenance of a constant internal environment.

Hormones control processes that need constant adjustment.

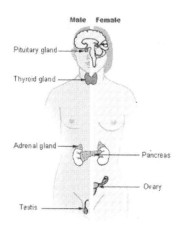

Target cells are cells within the target organ that have specific receptors on the membrane or in the cytoplasm for the hormone.

Once the hormone binds to the receptor, the target cells produce a response.

B3.3.2: Negative Feedback

Negative feedback is an important type of control mechanism used in homeostasis.

A small change in one direction is detected by receptors and the effectors then work to reverse the change and restore the normal conditions.

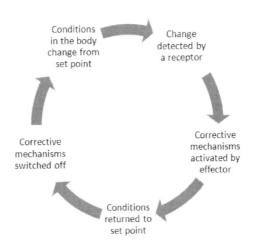

Conditions in the body change from set point

Change detected by a receptor

Corrective mechanisms activated by effector

Conditions returned to set point

Corrective mechanisms switched off

Thyroxine

Produced in the thyroid gland from iodine and tyrosine. It regulates the metabolic rate of the body.

The change in thyroxine levels is detected by the hypothalamus. If it is too low, the pituitary gland releases TSH. TSH travels in the blood to the thyroid gland where it stimulates the production of thyroxine. Once the hypothalamus detects the levels are back to normal, the pituitary stops making TSH and the thyroid stops making thyroxine.

A similar process happens with adrenaline which is made in the adrenal glands. It prepares the body for the 'fight or flight' response.

B3.2.3: The Menstrual Cycle

The cycle lasts about 28 days and prepares a woman's body for pregnancy.

Each month the lining of the uterus starts to thicken. At the same time, an egg starts to mature in one of the ovaries. About 14 days later, ovulation occurs (release of the egg).

The egg travels down the fallopian tube where it may be fertilised if sperm is present. The fertilised eff may implant in the uterus lining. This is where is receives all the nutrients and oxygen it needs as it develops.

If the egg is not fertilised, the uterus lining and egg are removed from the body. This is a period.

The menstrual cycle is controlled by four hormones:

1. Follicle Stimulating Hormones (FSH):
   - Secreted by the pituitary gland and travels to the ovaries in the bloodstream.
   - It causes an egg to mature and stimulates the production of oestrogen.

2. Oestrogen:
   - Made and secreted by the ovaries (corpus luteum) and causes the uterus lining to thicken.
   - Increasing oestrogen levels inhibit FSH production which usually stops more than one egg from maturing. It also stimulates the pituitary gland to release LH.

3. Luteinising Hormone (LH):
- Secreted by the pituitary gland.
- When LH levels peak, ovulation is triggered.

4. Progesterone:
- Produced by the ovaries (corpus luteum).
- Maintains the uterus lining, levels remain high throughout pregnancy.
- It also inhibits LH production.

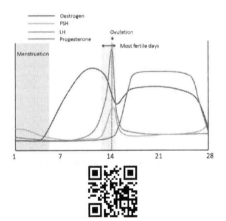

B3.2.4: Controlling Reproduction

Contraception: Any technique used to prevent pregnancy.

Two groups of contraception:

1. Hormonal: Uses hormones to disrupt the normal female reproductive cycle. E.g.
Combined pill, progesterone pill, IUS

2. Non-hormonal: Barrier methods that prevent the sperm reaching the egg or physical devices that release chemicals like spermicides. E.g.
Condoms, diaphragm, IUD

B3.2.5: Infertility Treatment

Infertility can be caused by:
- Blocked sperm ducts
- Not enough sperm being produced
- Lack of mature eggs
- Failure to release an egg

Hormones can be used to treat some of these conditions.

FSH can be used as a fertility drug as it stimulates eggs to mature in the ovaries so there is a greater chance of pregnancy.

IVF can be used if hormones alone do not help.

FSH and LH are given to the mother to ensure as many eggs as possible mature in her ovaries. These eggs are then collected and placed in a petri dish with sperm.

The eggs are then checked to ensure they have been fertilised and early embryos are implanted into the mother's uterus.

Considerations of IVF:
- Not natural
- Parents unable to have children naturally can conceive
- Older parents can have children
- Possibility of multiple births
- Very expensive
- Doesn't always result in pregnancy

B3.2.6: Plant Hormones

Tropism: Growth in response to an external stimulus. This allows plants to respond to their external environment.

Plants have a hormone called auxin which is made near the tips of roots and shoots.

Auxin stimulates shoot cells to grow more but inhibits the growth of root cells.

Phototropism (Response to light)

Positive phototropism: Grow towards the light (shoots)
Negative phototropism: Grow away from the light (roots)

Auxin is made in the tip and diffuses back. It accumulates on the shaded side. In shoots, it makes the cells elongate on that side so it bends towards the light.

Gravitropism (Response to gravity)

Positive gravitropism (roots): Grow in the same direction as gravity
Negative gravitropism (shoots): Grow in the opposite direction to gravity.

The auxin accumulates on the side closest to the ground. This makes shoots grow up and roots grow down.

B3.2.7: Uses of Plant Hormones

Auxins can be used to stimulate growth by causing cell elongation. They can also be used to regulate fruit development.

Ethene (gas) causes fruit to ripen by stimulating the conversion of starch into sugar.

Gibberellins promote growth, particularly stem elongation. They also end the dormancy of seeds and buds.

There are several uses of plant hormones: Killing weeds: Weed killers are selective herbicides which contain auxins. They kill broad leaved plants but not narrow leaved plants by making the weed grow too fast.

Promoting root growth: Rooting powders contain auxins which stimulate root growth in cuttings.

Delaying ripening: Auxin can be sprayed on fruit trees to delay ripening. This means the harvest can be collected at the same time and prevents fruit dropping off trees.

Ripening Fruit: Ethene is sprayed onto fruit trees to ripen fruit quicker to make it ready earlier in the growing season.

Parthenocarpy (Seedless fruit): Auxin is applied to unpollinated flowers which makes the plant produce seedless fruit.

Controlling Dormancy: Gibberellins or auxin can be used to trigger germination of seeds to allow them to be grown all year round.

Check Your Understanding

1. What is a hormone?

2. Explain how negative feedback works.

3. Name the hormones involved in the menstrual cycle.

4. Describe the changes in hormones during the menstrual cycle and their effects.

5. Describe how IVF is carried out.

6. List the ways hormones are used in plants.

7. Explain how shoots always grow towards the light.

B3.3.1: Controlling Body Temperature

Normal human body temperature is 37°C. This is the optimum temperature for out enzymes to work at.

If we get too cold our core body temperature drops and enzyme reactions occur too slowly. Respiration does not release enough energy and cells die. If core body temperature drops below 35°C, you are at risk of hypothermia.

If we get too hot and our core body temperature rises above 40-42°C, the enzymes may denature.

We have receptor cells in the skin that monitor external temperature and internal receptor cells that monitor the temperature of your blood. This information is sent to the thermoregulatory centre in the brain.

When you are too hot:

- Body hairs lie flat against the skin to prevent air being trapped.
- Sweat glands produce sweat which transfers heat energy to the surroundings as water evaporates.
- Vasodilation occurs to increase blood flow through the capillaries so more heat is lost via radiation.

When you are too cold:

- Body hairs rise to trap air.
- Stop producing sweat.
- Vasoconstriction occurs (blood vessels narrow) to reduce blood flow through the capillaries so less heat is lost via radiation.
- Shivering to make cells respire faster and transfer extra energy.

B3.3.2: Controlling Blood Sugar

Glucose is released from your food during digestion. It moves from the small intestine to the bloodstream.

If levels of glucose remain high for an extended period, damage may occur to nerves and blood vessels.

The pancreas detects when blood sugar levels are too high and releases insulin into the blood. The insulin travels to the liver and triggers the conversion of glucose into glycogen for storage.

If blood sugar levels are too low, the pancreas releases glucagon which triggers the liver into converting glycogen into glucose.

If you cannot control your blood glucose level, you are said to have diabetes. There are two types:

Type 1: Cannot produce insulin as the immune system has destroyed pancreatic cells that make it. Normally starts in childhood and is controlled by insulin injections, balanced diet and exercise.

Type 2: Cannot effectively use insulin as not enough is made or the cells don't respond to it properly. This has links to obesity and starts later in life. It is controlled by eating a balanced diet and exercise but drugs may be given to stimulate insulin production or insulin injections given.

B3.3.3: Maintaining Water Balance

Excretion: Process by which waste products are removed from the body.

If too much water is in your blood plasma, the blood cells will burst.

If too little water is present in your blood plasma, the blood cells will shrink.

The main excretory product linked to water control is urine. Urine is a solution containing water, urea (toxic) and other waste substances. The urea is filtered out of the blood by the kidneys and then stored in the bladder.

The volume of urine you produce is dependent on how hydrated you are.

B3.3.4: The Kidney

The kidney has three sections:
1. Capsule: Outer membrane which helps keep the kidney shape and protect it from damage.
2. Cortex: Outer part of the kidney
3. Medulla: Inner part of the kidney

The kidney is made of nephrons. The top part is in the cortex and the lower part is in the medulla.

Blood enters the kidney under high pressure through the renal artery. Each branch of the renal artery leads to a glomerulus (knot of capillaries).

The blood vessel narrows at the exit to the glomerulus so blood pressure is increased. This forces small molecules out of the capillary and into the Bowman's capsule. This is ultrafiltration.

As the filtrate moves through the nephron tubule, all the glucose is reabsorbed as well as some water and any salts needed by the body. This is selective reabsorption.

The filtrate then passes through the loop of Henlé and the collecting ducts, where extra salt and water is reabsorbed.

The waste solution travels to the bladder, down the ureter, where excretion occurs.

Negative feedback is used to control the volume of urine made through the use of the hormone ADH. ADH makes the walls of the collecting ducts more permeable. It is released when water concentration in the blood is too low to increase water reabsorption.

B3.3.5: Osmotic Challenges

You need to drink about 2L of water a day.

If there is a reduction in water potential of the blood plasma, your body's thirst response is triggered.

This means a message goes to the brain to tell you to drink and the kidneys produce less urine.

Ignoring this may lead to dehydration which causes headache, dizziness and lack of energy. Long term dehydration can lead to kidney damage and death.

An excess of water can lead to lysis of cells. It can also cause muscle cramps, seizures and confusion as a result of lower sodium ion concentration. If water moves into brain cells, it may lead to death.

Check Your Understanding

1. Explain how your body responds when too hot.

2. Name the hormones involved in regulating blood glucose concentration.

3. Explain how blood glucose levels are controlled.

4. Name the 3 parts of the kidney.

5. Explain how the kidney works.

6. Explain what happens if you are dehydrated.

About Wright Science

Wright Science is a YouTube channel created by Vicki Wright, a secondary science teacher in England.

I started Wright Science as a resource for my own classes to have extra help outside of school time. It started with a single recap video for each exam back in 2013 and then just grew. These days there are videos for every lesson on both the separate science courses and combined science courses which are used by a number of students across the country and world!

I hope that you find this book useful and welcome your comments.

Good luck in your exams!

Printed in Great Britain
by Amazon